Bayside Pr

STUDENT ~ ~ ~

TO THE GREAT

COMPOSERS

A Guide to Music History for Students

by L. Dean Bye

Some illustrations by Barb Kimker-Furry

2

CONTENTS

THE PRE-RENAISSANCE PERIOD
(Before 1450)

Music has been a part of our lives for thousands of years. In fact, there are pictures and writings which tell about music as far back as 4,000 years before the time of Christ. Even in ancient times, people evidently made music of some type almost on a daily basis. It was found in places of worship, in homes; people used music for marching and for work. Thousands of years before the time of Christ, we have evidence that there were choirs of singers who were often accompanied by instrumentalists.

Music was important in the lives of the people in most ancient countries. Music, in fact, was often known as "the language of the gods" and was held sacred. Because of this, we find that sometimes only the priests were allowed to sing and play.

From the Bible, we are able to learn a great deal about the music of the ancient Hebrew people. King David himself was a musician and appointed one tribe of his people to be the "official musicians" of his government. Can you imagine 120 priests blowing trumpets while 4,000 musicians were playing cymbals, harps, psalteries—and at the same time singing? The Bible records such an event. What an impressive experience that must have been!

To some early people, music was magic. It was sung both as a lament for the dead or to celebrate a great victory. As a matter of fact, these people of 3,000 years ago probably used music in about as many ways as we do today.

Specifically, in early Greece, music was always used for feasts and festivals. (The word "music" comes from the Greek "muses.") Thousands of people traveled to music centers each year so that they might hear the great festivals. As a part of the Greek plays, there was a chorus of musicians. There were instrumentalists and, often, soloists. History also shows that the Greeks had professional dancers, as well.

Before we turn completely to the more modern periods of music history, we need to explore briefly the music of the Christian Church from the 4th century on. During the Dark and Middle Ages, the Church was basically in control of all of the arts, including music.

 Music, in fact, has always played an important part in the services of the Church. In the early Church, all music was vocal; and the purpose of the melody was to support the meanings of the words. Gregorian Chant, or plainsong, was composed as a

The history of music & harmony seems to follow the harmonic series C C 8ve the C G -5th the G C 4th the C E G triad the Bb 7th, then up chromatically C C#D etc.

9/20

single-line chant (melody) to be sung in unison without any type of harmony to support it. The rhythm of Gregorian Chant is a free rhythm—similar to speaking to music.

Gregorian Chants, which have been preserved in hundreds of manuscripts, are among the great treasures of Western civilization and stand as a monument to man's religious faith. During the later Middle Ages (from the 9th century on), other voice parts were added to the original chant melodies. This was the beginning of polyphony (many melodies). This type of musical treatment of the Church service reached its highest point in the polyphonic music of Giovanni-Pierluigi da Palestrina, who we will discuss in our look at the Renaissance Period on the next page.

THE RENAISSANCE PERIOD

(1450 to 1600)

RENAISSANCE—"Re-birth." The artistic period called the Renaissance was a time during which a glorious flowering of art and music occured. It was also a time of renewed interest in exploring all aspects of living. Musically, vocal music was the most important, and polyphonic music (which we mentioned earlier) was emphasized. New ideas of rhythm and melody were explored. Techniques and mechanics of melody writing were combined, with attention given to the musical ideas and the beauty of the sound.

As was previously stated, the greatest composer of this period was Palestrina. He wrote in almost every style available to him, and his works were often used as models by other composers. No one before Palestrina had brought to music so much beauty and attention to musical detail.

Even though we have talked mostly about the music of the Church (see page 4), the polyphonic music of the Renaissance was not all religious. In the 16th century, secular (non-religious or "popular") polyphonic music came into being. It was livelier and more rhythmic than the music of the Church. The <u>Madrigal</u> was one of these early types of "music for fun."

The "point to remember" when discussing the music of the Renaissance is the importance of <u>polyphony</u> (many melodies). It is this combination of a number of melodies overlapping by entering and leaving at various times which separates Renaissance music from that which was to come later.

GIOVANNI-PIERLUIGI
DA PALESTRINA

GIOVANNI-PIERLUIGI DA PALESTRINA

(1525 to 1594)

Palestrina received his name from the small Italian town near Rome in which he was born in 1525. As a young boy, he sang in the cathedral choir of his native town; but as he became more skilled, he transferred to the choir-school of St. Maria Maggiore in Rome. In 1539 when his voice changed, Palestrina left the choir-school and returned home.

In 1544 he was appointed organist and choir master of the cathedral in his native town. Shortly after, he married and eventually became the father of two sons. About 1551, the Pope made him the choir master of the Julian Chapel at the Vatican. In 1554, Palestrina published a book of Masses, dedicated to the Pope. For this, Palestrina was rewarded by being made a member of the Pope's private chapel choir in 1555. He served only six months in this choir, as a change of popes occurred; and he was dismissed because of a rule against married singers. In 1571 he became Maestro of the Cappella Giulia, retaining this position until his death.

In 1584, Palestrina brought out his settings of "The Song of Solomon," and his harmonized version of the Latin Hymnal was published. His Mass entitled "Pope Marcellus Mass" was considered to be his best work and was used as a standard by which all other works of this type were judged. He died in 1594 and was buried in the Cappella Nuova of old St. Peter's.

Although Palestrina's music was always sung in the Sistine Chapel in the Vatican, it otherwise fell into general neglect for almost 200 years after his death. In the 1800s, a revival of interest began; and modern editions of his music were published.

Composers before Palestrina seemed to hold very strictly to the prevailing rules of composition. Although Palestrina knew the rules, the <u>beauty</u> of the composition was his first thought. Of course, Palestrina's many works were all polyphonic, the style of writing that was so very important in the music of the Renaissance Period.

THE BAROQUE PERIOD
(1600 to 1750)

The Baroque Era was a time of magnificence and splendor in architecture, music, and art. It was also a time of intense religious feeling and a time of devastation and destruction in Europe. (Germany was involved in the 30 Years War.)

Art and music were supported largely by wealthy nobility and by the Church. Noblemen and clergymen were both well educated, and they were interested in the arts and sciences. The ruling families throughout Europe were responsible for much of the cultural development during this time.

In fact, artists and musicians could not have existed without being paid by a wealthy nobleman or official of the Church. Artworks were frequently created for a specific purpose, either to decorate a building or for a special occasion. The arts, therefore, fulfilled a practical purpose and gave artistic pleasure, as well.

George Frederic Handel, one of the leading composers of the Baroque Period, was often commissioned by King George I of England to compose music for special social events. It was common for London newspapers to mention Handel on both the society pages and the pages devoted to news.

German church music of the Baroque Period was greatly influenced by chorales (or hymns) of the German Protestant Church.
Many of these tunes were melodies the people already knew
placed with words that were more suitable for the church service. These hymns were usually harmonized so that they could be
sung in parts by both choirs and congregations. Johann Sebastian Bach was one of many Baroque composers who wrote
hymns and chorale tunes for the Church.

George Frederic Handel and Johann Sebastian Bach were two of
the most important composers of the Baroque Era. During this
period, as in the Renaissance, musicians were thought of as
servants; nevertheless, they enjoyed a certain independence
since musicians were also frequently organized into musician
guilds.

The guilds regulated training and worked to uphold the rights of
their members. Through the guilds, standards of excellence
were maintained in the musical profession. Both Bach and
Handel were members of the guilds and followed their training
schedule to become master musicians. These two composers
created many of the outstanding musical masterpieces from this
period of history.

SOME GENERAL CHARACTERISTICS OF BAROQUE MUSIC ARE:

MELODY: A single melodic idea.

RHYTHM: Continuous rhythmic drive.

TEXTURE: Balance of homophonic (melody with chordal harmony) and polyphonic textures.

TIMBRE: Orchestral—strings, winds (and harpsichord) with very little percussion. *continuo*

DYNAMICS: Abrupt shifts from loud to soft— achieved by adding or subtracting instruments.

An overall characteristic of Baroque music is that a single musical piece tended to project a single mood or expression of feeling.

grandiose concept
magnificent effects
contrasts
ornate design
overall theatrical quality

JOHANN SEBASTIAN BACH

JOHANN SEBASTIAN BACH
(1685 to 1750)

Bach was the first great musician to disregard the rules of harmony and rhythm that were strictly followed by other composers. This fact alone helped to make him the forerunner of musical composition as we know it today. Born the son of a violinist in Eisenach, Germany, in 1685, he received his first musical training on the violin.

At the age of 10, he went to live in the home of his brother, Christoph, who taught Johann to play the harpsichord and the organ. It was also at this time that Bach began school, where his boy-soprano voice was greatly admired and appreciated. When his voice changed, Bach concentrated on the violin; but the organ soon took his interest, and he decided to devote himself to church music.

At the age of 18, Bach became the organist at Arnstadt and began his work in musical composition. After a short period of time, he moved to Muhlhausen where he married his cousin, Maria Bach. At Muhlhausen he began to experiment with changes in the music used in the church services of the German Protestant Church. It was also during this time that he began to become somewhat well known. It was this that gained for him the position as court organist and violinist to the duke at Weimar, where he remained for about nine years.

During this nine-year period, he wrote many cantatas for the Church, suites for the clavichord and harpsichord, and fugues (musical compositions in which the first melody is continually repeated and imitated throughout the entire piece). In fact, because he wrote so many fugues for the organ and piano, he is often called "the Great Master of the Fugue."

His next position at Kothen was during the period in which he produced much of his orchestral music and music for the clavichord and harpsichord. In 1720 his wife died; and a year later he married Anna Wulken, who was also a musician. She evidently helped him considerably in his work. Notebook for Anna

In 1723 Bach went to Leipzig as music director of the Thomasschule. During his stay at Leipzig, he wrote many of his church cantatas and oratorios. Among these is his famous "Christmas Oratorio." In 1749 Bach became totally blind; and in the following year, 1750, he died.

Historians tell us that Bach did not seem to associate very much with other musicians and was far more interested in his family of 20 children and in composing and directing his church choirs than in becoming "famous." In addition to his almost unequaled skill as a composer, he also was an excellent organ builder, as well as an expert music copyist.

Since most of his life was spent within a few miles of his birth-
place, we also now know that Bach's music was not widely
known throughout the world during his lifetime. In fact, many
of Bach's most beautiful works were unpublished and unper-
formed for almost 100 years, until two later composers (Mendelssohn and Schumann) discovered the beauties of his music
and began to perform them and make them known to the world.

Major Works
Mass in B m~
St. Matthew Passion

Well-tempered Clavier

6 Concerto Grossi - Brandaburg.

18

GEORGE FREDERIC HANDEL

GEORGE FREDERIC HANDEL
(1685-1759)

George Frederic Handel was born at Halle, Germany, in 1685. His father, who was not a musician, wanted Handel to become a lawyer and opposed his desire to study music. Nevertheless, Handel, without his father's knowledge or approval, taught himself to play the harpsichord.

Finally, at the age of 7, his father allowed him to study music. Lessons were arranged; and, by the age of 11, Handel played the harpsichord, organ, violin, and oboe. By this time, he had also composed six sonatas for two oboes and bass and was the assistant organist to his teacher at Halle Cathedral.

In 1702 he entered Halle University and started studying law. However, he continued to hold a position as a church organist. One year later, Handel joined an orchestra in Hamburg; and, at the age of 20, he wrote his first opera, "Almira."

In 1707 Handel visited Italy and then wrote his first Italian opera. Shortly thereafter, the production of his opera "Agrippina" in Venice spread his fame throughout Italy.

Handel returned to Germany around 1710 to become choir master to the elector of Hanover, but shortly traveled to London, where a production of one of his operas was so successful that he was asked to remain in England. Handel decided to return to Germany; but, on his next visit to London in 1712, he wrote

among other things "An Ode for the Queen's Birthday," which
won him such public and royal favor that he was given an annual salary of several hundred pounds.

Within a very short period, his former employer, the elector of
Hanover, became King George I of England. Handel's famous
"Water Music" was written for George I for a festival on the
River Thames. The King so greatly enjoyed the music that, from
that time until he died, Handel received a salary from the Brit-
ish court.

In 1720 Handel was appointed director of the Royal Academy of
Music in London, where he produced a large number of operas.
Many of these works were considered "failures," so he finally
redirected his attention to oratorios and composed the works for
which he is now best known. Handel's oratorios were written
after he was 53 years old. The most famous of these, "Messiah,"
was written in less than a month's time.

At one of the first London performances of "Messiah," King
George I was so inspired by the "Hallelujah Chorus" that he
stood up. The entire audience followed his example, which
began the present custom of standing when the "Hallelujah
Chorus" is sung.

Handel became almost totally blind six years before his death, but continued to perform until he died. He was a naturalized British subject and, when he died in 1759, was buried in Westminster Abbey in London.

Major Works

THE CLASSICAL PERIOD

(1750 to 1825)

The term "Classical music" specifically refers to music written during a period of music history dating from about 1750 to 1825. Because much of the activity of the great classical composers—Haydn, Mozart, and Beethoven—centered around Vienna, Austria, it is often called the "Viennese-Classical Period." The Classical Period was an attempt to reject the highly complex and ornamented music and art of the Baroque Period. Classicism can best be described as having qualities of balance and order.

During the Classical Period, three great revolutions took place in the world: the Industrial Revolution, the American Revolution, and the French Revolution. The Industrial Revolution, triggered by the invention of the steam engine, stimulated manufacturing and commerce and enabled the middle class to gain wealth and influence. Both the American and French Revolutions were challenges to the ruling monarchies and served to improve the lot of the common man. By the end of the 18th century, the power of kings all over the world had been greatly reduced.

This change had its effect on musicians. At the beginning of the Classical Period, musicians were still dependent on the wealthy and the Church; and they were considered to be in the servant class. Gradually, this began to change; and, by 1800, composers were writing mainly for the general public.

The first of the great classical composers was Franz Joseph Haydn. In 1761 he began serving Prince Esterházy of Hungary. He remained in this position for almost 30 years.

Haydn had considerable freedom in writing music during this time, but other requirements were fairly severe. He was expected to behave as a servant, and it was his duty to produce any type of composition upon demand. Haydn was required to be present twice a day to receive orders; and it was his responsibility to discipline the orchestra, to copy all of the music, and to rehearse all of the musicians.

While Haydn worked as a servant to a prince, Wolfgang A. Mozart found this kind of life unbearable. At 25, he resigned from his position with the Archbishop of Salzburg, and from then on he attempted to earn a living from the sale of his music and from his public performances. Mozart never had much money, but he is credited with improving the status of the independent musician.

The third great classical composer was Ludwig van Beethoven. Beethoven was very independent and became the first composer to earn a living from the sale of his compositions. He regarded himself an equal of the nobility and wrote only compositions that he wanted to write.

The music of the Classical Period, as in all periods of history, reflects the society from which it comes. Life during the Classical Period was elegant and formal. The people dressed in elaborate clothes and wigs. The furniture and homes were designed for their formal beauty. It stands to reason, then, that the music of Haydn and Mozart, as well as the earlier compositions of Beethoven, tended to follow rather formal structures.

One of the most important forms of music to come into being during the Classical Period was the string quartet—that is, music written for first and second violin, viola, and cello. An important feature of these compositions was that none of them contained a part for the harpsichord. This was important because, in the Baroque Period, the harpsichord was almost always used to strengthen the harmony. The Classical string quartet was the string quartet as we know it today. Most of the major composers since that time have written for that particular medium.

SOME GENERAL CHARACTERISTICS OF CLASSICAL MUSIC ARE:

MELODY: Short and clearly defined musical phrases with two or more contrasting themes.

RHYTHM: Very defined and regular.

TEXTURE: Mostly homophonic. — melody with harmony

TIMBRE: The symphony orchestra was organized into four sections—strings, woodwinds, brass, and percussion. The harpsichord was very seldom used.

FRANZ JOSEPH HAYDN

FRANZ JOSEPH HAYDN
(1732 to 1809)

Franz Joseph Haydn was born in Rohrau, Austria, in 1732. By the age of 5, Haydn obviously had musical talent; and he was sent to study with a relative living close to Vienna. When Haydn was 8 years old, he became a member of the famous choir at St. Stephen's Cathedral in Vienna. For nine years he sang both at the cathedral and in the homes of the nobility.

When Haydn was dismissed from the choir at the age of 17, he turned to other forms of music. His main interest was the harpsichord and violin, but he also studied composition thoroughly. By the age of 27, he was well known throughout Vienna. It was during this period of his musical life that he wrote his first Mass and first string quartet.

Because he was so well known, Haydn caught the attention of the famous Hungarian noble family of Esterházy. Haydn was only 29 when he entered their service as the assistant conductor of the orchestra. Two years later he was made conductor. Under his direction, it soon became one of the finest private orchestras of that time.

In 1790 Prince Nikolaus Esterházy died, and Haydn was dismissed from service. He immediately visited London for the purpose of giving a series of concerts. He was received with such enthusiasm that Oxford University conferred on him an Honorary Doctorate of Music. Some of his best orchestral works were

No 101

written during this time in England. "The Clock," "The Surprise," and "The London" are today considered some of the best of his symphonies.

In 1795 Haydn returned to Austria and was honored throughout the country. It was not long after this that he wrote "The Emperor's Hymn," which became the Austrian national anthem. He continued writing until his death in 1809.

It was Haydn's achievement in the instrumental-music field that earned for him his place in music history. In fact, he has often been called "the Father of the Symphony" because his symphonic works so overshadowed the works of those who came before him.

Major Works

WOLFGANG AMADEUS MOZART

WOLFGANG AMADEUS MOZART
(1756 to 1791)

Wolfgang Amadeus Mozart, born at Salzburg, Austria, in 1756, began taking lessons from his musician father at age 4; and at age 5 he began to compose. Mozart learned so quickly that in 1762 his father took him to Munich and Vienna to introduce him to the public. In Vienna, Mozart played before the emperor of Austria. It was at this same time that Mozart learned to play the violin without any instruction. It is also said that he did the same thing on the organ after someone explained the use of the pedals to him.

The following year, when Mozart was 7, the entire family traveled to Paris, where he had his first compositions published. Mozart traveled almost constantly. Before he was 25 years old, he had visited most of the great cities of Europe.

In 1764, while visiting in England, he composed several sonatas for violin and harpsichord and a number of symphonies. Mozart was only 8 years old. In 1769, on a visit to Rome, history tells us that Mozart went to hear the Sistine choir sing; and, after returning home, he put the entire work on paper from memory.

Mozart's father was in service to the Archbishop of Salzburg most of his life, so Mozart was appointed concert-master to the archbishop for a short time. Mozart was never able to accept the role of servant very well, however; so, after a number of differences of opinion, he was dismissed in 1781. From then on, he was basically "on his own."

In 1782 he married Constance Weber, the cousin of another great composer, Carl Maria Von Weber. It was during their life together, much of which was spent in poverty, that his three great operas, "Don Giovanni," "The Magic Flute," and "The Marriage of Figaro," were written. The writing of his last work, "The Requiem," was not finished at his death. Mozart died in Vienna and was buried in a "pauper's grave," the exact spot not known.

Mozart's productivity was astounding, and he wrote in virtually every style available to him. While his basic texture is homophonic (melody with chordal harmony) and very "harmonic," he was also excellent in polyphonic writing. His experience all over Europe and his contact with the different musical styles made his works typical of the entire European musical situation as it was during his lifetime.

Major works

LUDWIG VAN BEETHOVEN

LUDWIG VAN BEETHOVEN
(1770 to 1827)

Beethoven was born in 1770 in Bonn, the city on the Rhine River which is now the capital of West Germany. Both his grandfather and his father were professional musicians. Beethoven began music lessons in violin, piano, and composition with his father when he was 4 years old. This arrangement continued until he was 9. In addition to this, he attended the public school in Bonn until he was 14.

When he was quite young, Beethoven could improvise ("make up" music on the spur of the moment) very well on the piano; and in 1781 he composed his first published composition. A year later he began his first "paying job" as assistant court organist in Bonn. Beethoven also played second viola in both the theatre and church orchestras.

1787
At the age of 17, Beethoven met Mozart on a visit to Vienna. Mozart was so impressed with his ability to improvise and his performance skills that he supposedly said, "He will give the world something worth listening to."

In 1792 Haydn met Beethoven in Bonn and was extremely complimentary of his work. This so impressed the elector (the governor) that Beethoven was sent to Vienna to study. It was in Vienna that he took lessons from Haydn.

30
Around 1800, Beethoven began to notice that he was becoming deaf; and by 1820 his deafness had increased to the point that he

could no longer conduct his orchestra. Although completely deaf for the last seven years of his life, he continued to write. Some of his greatest compositions were produced during this time. He died in Vienna in 1827.

Beethoven wrote in practically all musical forms, but is one of the greatest of all instrumental composers. His works include one opera, an oratorio, two Masses, various songs, as well as sonatas for piano and for the violin. His concertos include five for the piano and one for the violin.

His nine symphonies are considered his greatest works. His ninth symphony was revolutionary in that he used a large choir with the orchestra in the last movement. On its first performance, the audience responded with wild applause; but Beethoven could not hear them. Only when the concert master turned him around did he see how enthusiastically it was received. It has been said that his third symphony was Beethoven's favorite, but his fifth symphony is the most popular today.

No. 1
No. 2
No. 3 - Eroica
No. 4
No. 5
No. 6
No. 7 -
No 8
No. 9 - Choral

THE ROMANTIC PERIOD

(1825 to 1900)

The Romantic Period in music occurred during a time of great social, political, and economic change. As a result of the American Revolution, the French Revolution, and the Industrial Revolution, the whole structure of society was changed. From a society of farms and small cities where the wealth was held by the nobility and the Church, an industrial society of factories and cities grew. This new society was controlled by "the new middle class." No longer did a man have to be a servant unless he chose to be one. Now he could raise himself up as high as his own abilities an initiative would take him.

The Romantic ideas spread throughout Europe and influenced both art and music. Instead of emphasizing logic and controlled emotions, the "Romantics" placed a great importance on personal feelings and emotions. They were interested in the unusual and the fantastic. Romantic composers were concerned with self-expression, and they felt that the Classical forms were too binding for them. Consequently, they either created new forms or changed those that were used before.

Romanticism found expression in many musical forms which included the symphony, the concerto, the opera, the art song, the solo piano piece, and the symphonic poem. One of the most characteristic Romantic forms was the <u>art song</u>, and the great Romantic composer who was known for his art songs was Franz Schubert. Few composers have had Schubert's gift for melody. He believed a song should express emotions both through the words and the music.

The piano was the favorite instrument of many Romantic composers because it was an instrument on which some of the distinctive qualities of Romantic music could be expressed. One of the greatest composers of piano music during the 1800s was Frederick Chopin, who wrote almost entirely for this instrument. Chopin explored the piano's possibilities through his preludes, waltzes, etudes (studies), and impromptus with remarkable originality. He developed a harmonic and a melodic style that strongly influenced composers for years after his death.

In short, the Romantic Period in music was exciting and revolutionary. Probably more than half of the serious music heard in concert halls today comes from composers of this period of music history. New styles of compositions became the norm and indeed continue to dominate today's concert halls. In the opinion of many, the Romantic Period was the "Golden Age" of concert music.

SOME GENERAL CHARACTERISTICS OF ROMANTIC MUSIC ARE:

MELODY:
Long, lyrical melodies with irregular phrases;
wide, somewhat angular skips;
extensive use of chromaticism;
vivid contrasts;
a variety of melodic ideas within one movement.

RHYTHM: Frequent changes in both tempo and meter.

TEXTURE: Almost entirely homophonic.

TIMBRE:
A great variety of tone color;
woodwind and brass sections of the orchestra increased;
many special orchestral effects introduced;
rich and colorful orchestration.

FRANZ SCHUBERT

FRANZ SCHUBERT
(1797 to 1828)

Franz Schubert was born in 1797 near Vienna. His family was
rather poor, since his father was a schoolmaster. Schubert
received his first musical instruction from his father, an ama-
teur cellist, and was taught violin beginning at the age of 8. By
the time he was 11, he began lessons on the piano, organ, and in
voice. In fact, Schubert's voice was so beautiful that he was
quickly admitted into the Imperial Choir and the training school
for the court singers. In this school, he was taught theory and
was the first violinist in the orchestra. Occasionally, Schubert
was allowed to conduct.

After studying instrumental composition, he wrote his first
symphony in 1813. The following year he completed his first
Mass (1814). In order to escape being forced into the military,
he took a job as elementary teacher in his father's school. It was
during these years that he began to compose with great rapidity.
His entire "leisure" time was devoted to composition. In 1815 he
wrote his famous art song, "Erl King." In 1816 he left the school
and went to Vienna, where he spent the remainder of his life.

Schubert's fondness for parties, his unbusinesslike habits, and
his lack of attention to day-to-day living made his life a struggle
for existence. Like Beethoven, Schubert never married; and,
beautiful as his music is, it was not appreciated during his lifetime. He died in Vienna at the age of 31 and was buried near
Beethoven, whom he greatly admired.

Schubert had the least formal training of all the great German musicians of his time, but his keen musical mind and his fantastic melodic gift made up for the lack of formal education. He is famous as the creator of German art songs, of which he wrote over 600. Two of his best-known art songs are "Serenade" and "Ave Maria." Many people feel that he contributed more to the development of the art song than any other composer in history.

Schubert wrote several dramatic works but was not overly successful in this style. He also wrote chamber music and piano music, as well as for choir. He composed eight symphonies, the most famous one being the "Unfinished Symphony." This symphony was never performed during Schubert's lifetime and is "unfinished" only in the sense that it has only two movements instead of the normal four.

His "Symphony in C Major," which some consider his greatest, was never heard by the composer, either. It was not until 11 years after his death that it was performed under Felix Mendelssohn.

FELIX MENDELSSOHN

FELIX MENDELSSOHN
(1809 to 1847)

Born in Hamburg, Germany, in 1809, the son of a wealthy
banker, Felix Mendelssohn had none of the financial worries
common to many other famous composers. Like Mozart and
Beethoven, his musical talent was noticeable at an early age.
Everything possible was done to give him the best of training.
Felix first received instruction on the piano from his mother and
also studied theory and violin. By the time he was 10, Mendelssohn played in public. At 12 he could compose remarkably
well.

When Felix was only 17, he wrote an overture to Shakespeare's
"A Midsummer Night's Dream," which is thought by some to be
the most beautiful musical work written by anyone that young.
His first and only real opera was performed in Berlin in 1827.
In 1829, with the performance of the "St. Matthew Passion," he
drew attention to Bach's compositions, as this was the first
performance of Bach's works anywhere since his death in 1750.

At about this time, Mendelssohn made his first trip to England
and not only conducted his "Symphony in C Minor" as well as a
number of other major works, but also established himself as an
excellent pianist and a fine organist. Following this concert
season, Mendelssohn began a series of tours which took him to
Scotland, Austria, Germany, Italy, Switzerland, and then to
Paris, France.

It is generally acknowledged that Mendelssohn was one of the first to write independent concert overtures. Before this, overtures were written as musical introductions to operas or oratorios, while the concert-overture, as developed by Mendelssohn, is complete in itself.

From 1833 to 1835, Mendelssohn conducted important festivals throughout Germany. In 1835 he became conductor of the famous Gewandhaus Orchestra. He married in 1837 (and became the father of five children), and in 1843 he founded the Leipzig Conservatory—one of the most famous of all music schools. In 1846, while in England, Mendelssohn conducted his most famous oratorio, "Elijah." He was greatly admired by the English and is considered to have made a greater impression on English music than any other composer, with perhaps the exception of Handel.

On returning from a trip to England in 1847, Mendelssohn learned of his sister's death—a shock from which he never recovered. He died shortly in Leipzig and was buried in Berlin.

His music, filled with original beauty and clearness of melodic expression, consists of symphonies, overtures, concertos, music for different combinations of string instruments, piano compositions, organ music, and his famous oratorios "St. Paul" and "Elijah."

FREDERIC CHOPIN
(1810 to 1849)

Frederic Chopin was born in 1810 in a small village near War-
saw, Poland. His father conducted a private school for sons of
the Polish nobility. It was here that Chopin began his general
education. Although he did study music with professional teachers, he was in a sense self-taught. When he was only 9 years
old, his talent was so pronounced that Chopin played a piano
concerto in public. While still very young, he appeared as a
pianist in various German cities. His first published work (in
1825) was a rondo (a composition consisting of one principle
theme which appears again and again, alternating with other
themes).

In 1829, already a composer who was somewhat known and a
polished player, Chopin set out for London by way of Vienna,
Munich, and Paris. His first concert in Paris was given to a
select audience of musicians who were so impressed that he did
not go on to London. He remained in Paris for the remainder of
his life. Not only did Chopin make a deep and lasting impression in Paris, but he was a very close friend of men like Franz
Liszt, as well as other famous musicians and artists. He was
admitted to their circle as a valued and equal companion.

From the beginning of his life in Paris, he taught piano. Chopin
had an intense dislike for public concerts, so his yearly concerts
were for the musical elite only. Occasionally, he would play in
certain private homes. Robert Schumann, reviewing some of his

works in 1839, wrote a glowing article in which he praised Chopin highly. His position in both society and the music world was secure.

Chopin, through Liszt, first met the novelist George Sand in 1836 and fell deeply in love. He believed she was the source of his inspiration. In 1838 he developed a severe case of bronchitis from which he never recovered. While fighting to keep from dying, Chopin worked hard at composing. When his sickness turned into tuberculosis, he and George Sand parted. Disregarding his failing health, Chopin visited Great Britain in 1848 and again in 1849. These trips exhausted him completely. Very sick and depressed, he returned to Paris in 1849 to die.

To Chopin goes much credit for treating the piano as a solo instrument. His music, as none before, uses pure piano-tone. His scherzos, ballades, preludes, nocturnes, and concertos show a peak in piano writing which has never been surpassed.

Chopin was dreamy and poetical. His music, mostly written for the piano, expressed his thoughts and feelings. Its sadness was probably the outcome of his brooding over the destruction of Poland. Occasionally, perhaps because of his life in Paris, his music portrayed happiness and tenderness. His playing was perfect; his technique brilliant; and the interpretation of his own works outstanding. Chopin was the perfect Romanticist.

FRANZ LISZT

FRANZ LISZT

(1811 to 1886)

Franz Liszt, famous pianist and composer, was born in Hungary
in 1811, the son of a steward on one of Prince Esterhazy's estates. Liszt began studying piano at the age of 6 with his father.
Franz's progress was so rapid that, at the age of 9, he played his
first public concert. The family moved to Vienna in 1821, where
Franz studied piano and theory—composing a considerable
number of short church pieces. When he was only 11, he gave a
concert which won great praise from Beethoven. It is said
Beethoven was so impressed with Liszt's performance that he
asked to see him personally.

These Viennese concerts were so successful that the elder Liszt
decided to take Franz to Paris to study at the Conservatory.
Admission was refused, though, because of a rule forbidding the
entrance of foreigners. However, Liszt continued to study composition. In fact, his only operetta was produced at this time.
By then he was a well-known pianist, and the next two years
were spent in concert tours.

His father's death in 1827 forced Liszt to support his mother and
himself. He decided to settle in Paris, where he was in great
demand as a teacher. When he was 28, Franz set out on a concert tour of Europe, which brought him not only recognition as
the greatest pianist of his day, but also considerable wealth.

In 1849 Liszt accepted the position of music director of the court
at Weimar, which he held for ten years. Liszt always did a lot

with the works of other composers, which also gained for himself additional fame as a great conductor. At this time, Weimar became a center for musicians of all types.

The next period of his life was spent in Rome, where he studied for the Church. In 1866 the Pope conferred on him the title of Father. The remainder of his life was spent in Rome, with several months of each summer spent at Weimar. While attending a Wagner festival at Bayreuth in 1886, Liszt was taken quite ill and died a few weeks later.

Liszt's life may be divided into two periods. The first was that in which he devoted himself almost exclusively to the piano. Most of his original piano works and his transcriptions and arrangements on works of other composers belong to this period.

The second period started with the ten years of Weimar. Here he devoted himself to composition in the larger forms. His own symphonic poems were written during this time. In fact, most people give him credit for begin the creator of the symphonic poem (a musical setting of a story, free in style—and usually in only one movement). The Hungarian rhapsodies, his cantatas, piano concertos, Masses, and short works for orchestra and piano were composed during these later years.

JOHANNES BRAHMS

JOHANNES BRAHMS

(1833 to 1897)

Brahms, born in Hamburg, Germany, came from a family which for generations had been interested in music. Brahms's father, a musician himself, gave Brahms his first musical instruction. Brahms was a willing and earnest student who at the age of 14 made his piano debut—playing his own variations on a folk song.

When he was 20, Brahms made a concert tour with violinist Remenyi. It was on this tour that he met Robert Schumann. Brahms's talent so impressed Schumann that he wrote an article in an important music journal naming Brahms as "the coming hero among composers." Schumann and his wife, Clara, remained his lifelong friends.

For four years he held a position as music director at the court of a German prince. After that, Brahms lived in various places and made concert tours which brought him artistic and financial success. He finally settled in Vienna in 1878. From that time on, Vienna was his home; and he died there in 1897.

Brahms never married. In his youth he was a brilliant pianist, and his first published music was for piano. He wrote every type of music except opera. He was patient and worked endlessly on his compositions, as was exemplified by the fact that he worked ten years, off and on, on his first symphony. Brahms was 43 when his first symphony was published in 1877, and it created a great sensation.

Brahms wrote with amazing technical skill, but his handling of the instruments was criticized by some as being not of the highest degree. Some critics also thought that he stressed the perfection of musical form far too much. This fact led some to say that his music tended to be heavy and dead at times.

Among Brahms's works are his four symphonies, smaller orchestral pieces, concertos, chamber music, piano music, many art songs, choral works, and choral-orchestral compositions. His "German Requiem" was the work said by many to have established his fame.

PETER ILITCH TSCHAIKOVSKY

PETER ILITCH TSCHAIKOVSKY
(1840 to 1893)

Tschaikovsky was born in Russia in 1840. He received piano lessons from his fourth to his tenth year, but none of his teachers saw any future in music for him. He then studied law and was graduated from law school at the age of 19.

He disliked law, though, and thought it boring; so at the age of 22 he entered the conservatory at St. Petersburg, where he studied under Rubinstein. Rubinstein, in 1866, hired Tschaikovsky as a professor of harmony at his new conservatory which he opened in Moscow. Tschaikovsky's position at the conservatory gave him time to write his first few symphonies, as well as other shorter compositions.

Shortly after moving to Moscow, his strange friendship began with Nadejda von Meck—an elderly and wealthy widow. Mrs. von Meck commissioned him for works for which she paid huge fees. The two never met, but carried on their friendship through letters. Tschaikovsky spent considerable time at the different von Meck estates when Mrs. von Meck was not there.

Tschaikovsky was a very shy man, but in 1877 he decided to marry. His marriage ended shortly thereafter and was a complete and tragic failure. This failure sent him into a state of near nervous collapse, so he moved to Switzerland to recover. Mrs. von Meck then offered him an annual income, which left him free to compose and travel as he desired. His fourth symphony was composed soon after this incident and reflects his apparently happy mental state. in 1878 he became director of the Moscow branch of the Russian Music Society.

Tschaikovsky's first public appearance as a conductor came in 1887 when he gave a concert of his own works at St. Petersburg. The following year, the Russian czar also began a yearly allowance. In addition, this was the year in which he made his first tour—conducting concerts in Germany, Prague, Paris, and London. Tchaikovsky also visited America in 1891 and conducted a concert at the dedication of Carnegie Hall. Six other very successful concerts were given in several other American cities, as well. He died in 1893.

Although Tschaikovsky was Russian, his music was not limited to that which sounds Russian. His music tends to be more universal and has strange and fierce contrasts of mood. In addition, his orchestrations show an excellent understanding of the orchestra. Tschaikovsky composed many songs, some operas, ballet music, various types of orchestral works, and chamber music; but most agree that his fame stems from his symphonies.

JOHANN STRAUSS JR.
(1825 to 1899)

In the early part of the 19th century, Vienna became famous as "the city of the waltz." Notable among the composers and conductors who made this form famous was the Strauss family. Johann Strauss Jr. was the best known as one of the principle promoters of the waltz. He was born in Vienna in 1825.

His father, Johann Strauss Sr., known as "the father of the waltz," was a successful orchestra conductor and composer who did not want to have a professional rival in his own family. Therefore, young Johann was intended for a business career. In 1844, though, Johann Jr. appeared at a restaurant at Hietzing with his own orchestra. He was extremely successful, and his new waltzes were very popular. From then on, he was his father's most powerful rival.

Johann's father died in 1849; and, shortly after his death, Johann Strauss Jr. united his orchestra with that of his father and made a successful concert tour through Austria, Poland, and Germany. In 1863 Strauss married Henriette Treffz, and that same year was made conductor of the court balls in Vienna. This position he held until 1870, when he turned from dance music and began to compose operettas. "Die Fledermaus," produced in 1874, and "The Gypsy Baron," produced in 1885, are perhaps the most popular of these.

Strauss died in 1899 in Vienna, leaving behind him a wealth of beautiful music. His 500 waltzes are indeed proof of his being known as "the waltz king." Prominent among these are "The Beautiful Blue Danube," "Tales from the Vienna Woods," and "The Emperor Waltz," which are included in the repertoire of all leading orchestras today.

Strauss created a type of waltz which has since become world known as the Viennese waltz, a type of music which has grace, lightness, and beautiful melodies as its chief characteristics. His finest waltzes, some of which we have already mentioned, have never been surpassed.

ANTON DVORAK

ANTON DVORAK

(1841 to 1904)

Born in 1841, Anton Dvorak was the son of an innkeeper. It was at his father's inn that he spent his evenings listening to the musicians playing. Because Anton was so interested in music, his father sent him to the best local teachers and finally to Prague. Because of increased cost, Dvorak had to rely on his violin playing as a means of earning enough money to continue his study.

Anton was 32 before he really became known as a composer and did not become known in America until he was appointed to the post of director of the National Conservatory of New York in 1892. He returned to his native Bohemia in 1895 to accept the directorship of the Conservatory of Prague.

There are only a very few compositions of lasting value that have also enjoyed immediate and widespread popularity. Dvorak's "New World Symphony" (his fifth such work) is one of the few. Dvorak composed this symphony at Spillville, Iowa, in 1893. In December of that year, it was performed for the first time by the Philharmonic Society of New York, with the composer in attendance. In this symphony, Dvorak sought not to present a strict version of native American music, but rather to interpret the spirit of American folklore.

Anton Dvorak was an original and very powerful musical genius. In addition to the "New World Symphony," one of Dvorak's most well-known compositions is his "Humoresque." This he wrote as a piano number in his later years. As a transcription, it is in every violinist's repertoire. He also wrote seven symphonies, five symphonic poems, six overtures, a number of concertos, many orchestral pieces and ensembles, eight operas, an oratorio, much church music, and many, many songs. He was still head of the famous Prague Conservatory when he died in 1904.

THE IMPRESSIONIST PERIOD

(Approximately 1885 to 1910)

In the late 19th century, we find a few composers rebelling against the rules of Romantic music. This was due in part to the result of a political conflict. In 1870 France was defeated by Germany in the Franco-Prussian War. The French people reacted by turning away from everything German and by emphasizing everything French. The result was an entirely new kind of musical and artistic expression. This movement came to be known as <u>Impressionism</u>.

The German composers loved to express themselves in musical works on a grand scale—operas with large casts and symphonies that lasted more than an hour. The French, mainly through the musical works of Claude Debussy, revolted against "bigness" and tried to break many of the so-called "rules" of musical composition.

The Impressionist painters were concerned with changing light and color rather than with heroic subjects. Because of this, they used such subject matter as clouds, reflections in the water, and fog. Their work was marked by vague outlines and subtle color changes. The emphasis was on catching a quick impression rather than creating an exact likeness. Influenced by the French painters, Debussy attempted to translate some of their effects into music.

One of the techniques he used to capture a vague, dreamlike quality was to break down the feeling of attraction to a tonal center. Debussy used a scale in which all tones are the same distance apart. Consequently, in his "whole-tone scale," as he called it, no tone acts as a tonal center. (In other words, there is no "key.") In harmony, Debussy defied tradition and often moved his chords in parallel motion.

In many cases, Impressionist composers gave us an "impression" in music of what they saw or heard. We are exposed to a musical picture without the composer's telling us what it actually is. Some people have likened Impressionistic music to objects seen dimly through a fog or through a sheer curtain. In short, Impressionistic music establishes a mood or a feeling, rather than telling a story.

CLAUDE DEBUSSY

CLAUDE DEBUSSY
(1862 to 1918)

The search for a new musical style at the end of the 19th century was evident everywhere, but it seemed to show itself in France to a greater degree than in other areas. Claude Debussy was one of the most important figures in French music during this period. He wrote in the highly individual style we now call "the Impressionistic style." This means the expression through music of what one actually experiences or imagines.

Claude Debussy was born in France in 1862. It was while Claude was still very young that he was sent to the Paris Conservatory, where he won many prizes for sight singing, piano, and composition. At the age of 22, he was awarded the Grand Prix de Rome, which entitled him to study in Italy for three years. In Italy, Debussy had enough time to work on new ideas and his new style. However, the compositions he wrote during this time were severely criticized. After three years, he returned to Paris to teach and play the piano, as well as to continue his work at composition.

Most of the critics and professors of that day observed strict musical form and rules. They did not approve of Debussy's work because it was so far from the "regular music." The fact that he had developed beautiful pieces of music was not important to these critics. In 1894 Debussy wrote a tone poem, "The Afternoon of a Faun," which created much talk and a lot of criticism. In fact, during the following years, Debussy wrote many things of great significance. Some which are outstanding are: two volumes of "Preludes for Piano," "Images," "La Mer," "Nocturnes," and others.

Perhaps Debussy's most well-known composition, "La Mer (The Sea)," was first performed in 1905. These three orchestral sketches indicate the perception and imagination of Debussy, for his actual experience of the ocean was limited to a very few crossings of the English Channel. Early performances of "The Sea" brought forth the usual outbursts from friends and critics, expressing both their approval and disapproval. Time, though, has brought about an appreciation of what Debussy tried to reflect in his music.

The last years of Debussy's life were spent under physical and financial hardship. A victim of cancer, he kept on working; but his financial problems, brought on by World War I, caused him great stress. In 1918 he died. It was quite some time later, however, before France and the rest of the world realized that Debussy, one of France's greatest musicians, was no longer living.

THE CONTEMPORARY PERIOD

(1900 to Present)

Almost unbelievable developments in the sciences, occurring at an increasing rate, are changing mankind and where he lives. Exploration, discovery, and technological advances in mathematics, chemistry, physics, bacteriology, and in the other sciences are responsible for changing the nature of life in the 20th century. All of the arts, reflecting the society in which they exist, have also undergone radical changes and have taken many new directions.

For example, since 1900 and even before, there have been composers who gradually broke away from the rules of musical composition and used discordant harmony and irregular melodies in their writing. The form or style of composition changed, as well. In place of the symphony, many wrote symphonic poems which were less rigid in style. Composers began using special musical effects of all types. Some worked for realism while others worked with "abstract music"—music without a story—music which required a "thinking musician" to perform (or even to appreciate).

Both the sciences and the arts have undergone constant changes ever since the beginning of man, but the break with tradition in the last 80 or 90 years has been radical and very conspicuous. To understand the changes that music has undergone in the 20th century is almost impossible; but, by reading about the following three composers and their music, one can begin to determine the degree to which modern music is different from or similar to the music of previous periods. These composers basically used only the instruments that were available to composers in the 19th century, but in recent years the whole field of electronic music has changed the musical scene even more dramatically.

SOME GENERAL CHARACTERISTICS OF CONTEMPORARY MUSIC ARE:

(Contemporary compositions vary widely, so this is not a complete list; and not all of these characteristics are present in every composition.)

1. Fewer lyrical melodies than the music of former periods.

2. Dissonant harmonies.

3. Complex rhythms.

4. Percussiveness.

5. Greater use of woodwind, brass, and percussion instruments than in music of earlier periods.

6. The use of synthetic and electronic sounds.

GEORGE GERSHWIN

GEORGE GERSHWIN
(1898 to 1937)

George Gershwin was born in Brooklyn, New York, and had very little interest in music as a young boy. However, one day while playing ball, he heard Max Rosen playing the violin. Soon after that, George looked up the violinist and became his close friend.

The Gershwins bought a piano for George's older brother, Ira, but it was not long before George was the one who showed interest. When only 16, Gershwin got a job with the Remick Publishing Company and soon was writing many songs. He was not satisfied with his work, however, and went to Rubin Goldmark for further study in harmony. Shortly, he took a job with the publishing firm of Harms. In 1919, Al Jolson made his song "Swanee" a million-copy hit.

Gershwin, at the age of 22, began writing the music for George White's Scandals; was receiving commissions from England; and was one of the most popular composers of "Tin Pan Alley." In 1924, Paul Whiteman commissioned Gershwin to write a work for his 1924 concert at Aeolian Hall. This work, now known all over the world, is the famous "Rhapsody in Blue." Successful scores for many Broadway shows and for the Hollywood screen followed, as well as a piano concerto, an overture, and finally the opera "Porgy and Bess," which was performed in 1935 for the first time.

Gershwin died very suddenly in Hollywood in 1937. He collapsed in his studio, and it was found that he had a brain tumor. Even though he had an operation, he died shortly thereafter. Gershwin was known for his intense desire to bring the popular, "Tin Pan Alley"-style of writing into serious music.

AARON COPLAND

(1900 to   )

Copland was born in Brooklyn in 1900. At the age of 14, he began lessons on the piano. Two years later, he studied the fundamentals of harmony under Rubin Goldmark. Interested in becoming a composer of modern music, he decided to go to Europe for further study. Living and studying near Paris was exciting, and Copland became familiar with all the progressive trends in contemporary music.

Almost all of his early works were written in a jazz idiom, but Copland's works which are usually considered the most important and which are played most frequently are those written after 1935. With the introduction of "El Salon Mexico" in 1936, his style of writing revealed a definite change. This work was based on melodies he had heard on a visit to Mexico.

Later, Copland used American folk themes as a basis for several of his ballets such as "Rodeo," "Billy the Kid," and "Appalachian Spring." He heard the famous Philadelphia Orchestra with Charles Rains as narrator perform his inspiring "A Lincoln Portrait." In addition, Copland is the writer of a considerable amount of chamber music.

Aaron Copland is not only a composer, but is an important lecturer, teacher, and writer as well. He has done much to promote contemporary music and has also helped to promote other contemporary composers.

DMITRI SHOSTAKOVICH
(1906 to 1975)

Shostakovich, perhaps the best internationally known of the modern Russian composers, was born in 1906. The son of musical parents, he showed at an early age that he was unusually gifted in music.

In 1919 he entered the Leningrad Conservatory where he wrote a set of eight piano preludes, along with his first published work. At 19, Shostakovich completed his first "symphony," which still enjoys international acclaim. In fact, it is to this day probably Shostakovich's most popular work outside his own country.

Shostakovich has been a recipient of the Stalin Award; and his position in the Soviet Union was up and down, reflecting political changes. Shostakovich's music is versatile, and most of it is excellent. Some of his best works are his first, fifth, and ninth symphonies; his concerto for piano, trumpet, and string orchestra; and his piano quintet. Shostakovich died in Moscow in 1975.

INTO THE NEXT CENTURY

We have now traced the history of music through the composers of the Renaissance, Baroque, Classical, Romantic, and Contemporary Periods. We have discovered that music is everyone's language. In addition, we have found that often, when we play a tune or sing a song, we are unable to tell the nationality, the color, the religion, or the politics of the person who wrote it. Music is universal.

It is difficult to tell what the new classification will be for "modern" composers. Some are called Ultramodern or Avant Garde because they follow few, if any, rules. To some, their compositions sound like noise. However—who can tell what the next 50 or 100 years will provide in the field of music?

Looking back into past periods of composition, we find that people usually accept music several years after it is first written. For example, the music of Bach was not well known for almost 100 years after he wrote it. The lives of the men included in this book are still influencing our lives because of the music which they wrote.

As we see and hear computer music, the increasing use of synthesizers, pure electronic music, as well as much of our popular music, it becomes very clear that changes are coming extremely fast. Some of the new material will endure; much of it will not. Only time will tell.

Highly Recommended!

ABCDEFGHIJKLMNOPQRSTUVWXYZ
BCDEFGHIJKLMNOPQRSTUVW MB94057 A
CDEFGHIJKLMNOPQRSTUVWXYZAB
DEFGHIJKLMNOPQRSTUVWXYZABC
EFG BCD
FGH CDE
GH DEF
HI EFG
IJ GH
JK GHI
KL HIJ
LM JK
MN KL
NO LM

Bayside Press Presents

STUDENT'S
MUSICAL
DICTIONARY

by L. Dean Bye

OPQRSTUVWXYZABCDEFGHIJKLMN
PQRSTUVWXYZABCDEFGHIJKLMNO
QRSTUVWXYZABCDEFGHIJKLMNOP
RSTUVWXYZABCDEFGHIJKLMNOPQ
STUVWXYZABCDEFGHIJKLMNOPQR
TUVWXYZABCDEFGHIJKLMNOPQRS
UVWXYZABCDEFGHIJKLMNOPQRST
VWXYZABCDEFGHIJKLMNOPQRSTU
WXYZABCDEFGHIJKLMNOPQRSTUV
XYZABCDEFGHIJKLMNOPQRSTUVW

Bayside Press

BAYSIDE PRESS, P.O. BOX 66, PACIFIC, MO 63069

Bayside Press
P.O. Box 66, Pacific, MO 63069-0066

Highly Recommended!

STAFF•TREBLE•SPACE•FLAT•CLEF•B
•NOTES•CLEF•BASS•NOTES•PI MB94086 •
METER•RESTS•METER•RESTS•DYNA
•MEASURE•SHARP•MEASURE•SHARP
DU

Bayside Press Presents

STUDENT'S
GUIDE TO
MUSIC THEORY

A Book of Music Fundamentals for Students

by L. Dean Bye

BARLINE•RHYTHM•MINOR SCALE•
•HARMONY•MINOR SCALE•HARMON
INTERVAL•CHROMATIC•INTERV
•CHROMATIC•CHORD•MELODY•STAF
STAFF•TREBLE•SPACE•FLAT•CLEF•B
•NOTES•CLEF•   NOTES•PITCH•
METER•RESTS•   RESTS•DYNA
•MEASURE•SHA   URE•SHARP
DURATION•TE   RLINES•TE
•BARLINES•RHYTHM•MINOR SCALE•

BAYSIDE PRESS, P.O. BOX 66, PACIFIC, MO 63069

Bayside Press
P.O. Box 66, Pacific, MO 63069-0066

—NOTES—

The following pages have been left blank to provide space for class notes or the recording of additional information.)

—NOTES—

—NOTES—

—NOTES—